ANIMAL HOMES

McGraw-Hill
Children's Publishing
A Division of The **McGraw·Hill** Companies

This edition published in the United States in 2002 by
Peter Bedrick Books, an imprint of
McGraw-Hill Children's Publishing,
A Division of The McGraw-Hill Companies
8787 Orion Place
Columbus, OH 43240

www.MHkids.com

ISBN 0-87226-690-7

Animal Homes created and produced by

M^cRAE BOOKS

via de' Rustici, 5, Florence (Italy)
tel. +39 055 264 384
fax +39 055 212 573
e-mail: mcrae@tin.it

Copyright © McRae Books Srl, 2001

Project Manager: Anne McRae
Graphic Design: Marco Nardi
Illustrations: Paola Holguín, Antonella Pastorelli, Ivan Stalio
Picture Research: Elzbieta Gontarska
Editing: Alison Wilson
Layout and cutouts: Adriano Nardi, Laura Ottina, Filippo Delle Monache

Color separations: Litocolor (Florence)
Printed and bound by Artegrafica, Verona, Italy

TROPICAL
RAIN FORESTS

Text by Anita Ganeri
Illustrations by Paola Holguín

PETER BEDRICK BOOKS

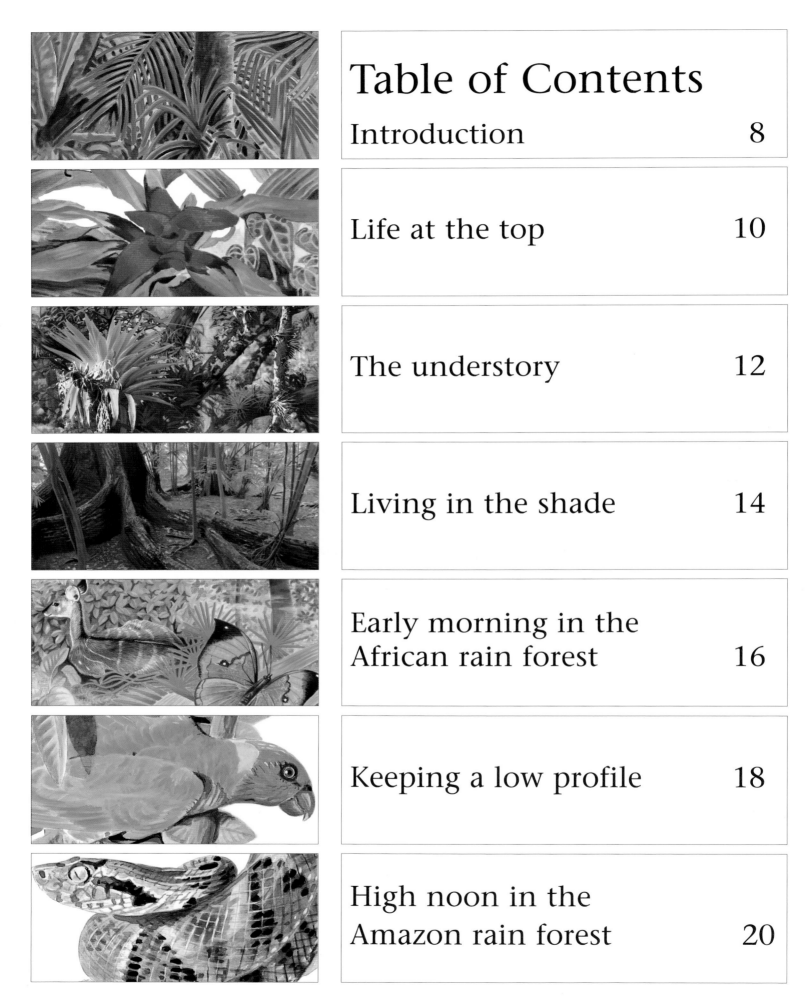

Table of Contents

Introduction

Rain forests, or jungles, grow along the equator, where it is hot, wet, and steamy all year round. They cover only about a sixth of the earth's surface but are home to millions of plants and animals, more than any other habitat. Scientists think that many more species are yet to be discovered. Rain forests are also home to many tribal peoples who rely on the forests for their food, materials, and livelihoods.

Orchid

Parrot

No change
The first rain forests grew about 150 million years ago, and they have not changed much since. A huge variety of plants and animals have evolved in this stable environment.

Tropical rain forests occur in regions with high rainfall and hot and steamy climates. The map shows the locations of the main rain forests in the world.

Plant life
The thick tangle of trees in the rain forest canopy stays green all year round. Vines twist around their trunks, and colorful flowers are continually in bloom.

THE ARCTIC

NORTH AMERICA

EUROPE · ASIA

ATLANTIC OCEAN

AFRICA

PACIFIC OCEAN

SOUTH AMERICA

INDIAN OCEAN

AUSTRALIA

Animal life
The constant warm temperature makes the rain forest an ideal home for many animals. The year-round plant growth means food is plentiful. Many animals live on flowers and leaves, or on the insects that feed on them. About half of all the known species of animals in the world live in rain forests.

Monkey-eating eagle (southeast Asia)

Cross-section of a rain forest

Rain forests grow in layers, depending on the height of the trees. Each layer is inhabited by its own typical plants and animals.

Emergents

The tallest trees in the rain forest are called emergents. Their tops poke out above the canopy. Huge monkey-eating eagles nest in the treetops and swoop down through the branches.

Loris (southeast Asia)

Canopy and understory

The canopy forms a thick, green roof over the rain forest. About two-thirds of jungle animals live in the canopy. Below it grow the palms and saplings of the understory.

Mandrill (Africa)

Forest floor

The forest floor is dark and gloomy because very little sunlight shines through the trees. The ground, where smaller creatures live, is littered with decaying leaves.

Rivers and streams

Rivers and streams snake across the forest floor, providing homes and food for many animals, such as tapirs, that are expert swimmers. Alligators and caimans lurk near the river bank, on the lookout for fish and mammals to eat. Many rain forest fish feed on fruit that falls into the river from the overhanging trees.

Alligator (South America)

Apes and monkeys
Many monkeys and apes, like this orangutan from southeast Asia, live in the canopy trees. They are so well-suited to their treetop homes that they rarely come down to the ground. They have long, strong arms for gripping onto branches and swinging through the trees.

Epiphytes
In the canopy, plants called epiphytes, or "air-plants," grow high up on the branches of the trees. They include plants such as orchids and bromeliads.

Life at the top

The trees of the canopy form a thick, green umbrella of leaves over the rain forest. A few very tall emergent trees poke up above the rest. The canopy, a dense mass of branches, leaves, flowers, and fruit, is warm and wet because it gets most of the sun and rain. Because it offers plenty of food and shelter, it is filled with rain forest animals. Each tree is home to hundreds of creatures, from tiny ants and beetles, to frogs, birds, and great apes.

CROSS-SECTION OF A RAIN FOREST

Emergents

Canopy

Plants and trees
With its air-plants and climbing vines, a canopy tree may support as many as thirty other plant species.

Iguana climbers

Using its long, sharp claws for gripping, the iguana from South America is a superb climber. Iguanas lay their eggs on the forest floor. When the young hatch, they climb up to live among the trees of the canopy and understory.

Emergent trees

Towering above the forest floor, some of the giant emergent trees can grow as tall as a twenty-story building. Their great height means that they get battered by howling winds and struck by lightning.

Life in the canopy

Most canopy animals have special features to help them survive among the trees. Flying squirrels from Asia glide through the branches using flaps of skin between their front and back legs as furry wings. Many insects have dappled patterns or green coloring on their bodies. This makes it harder for hungry birds or reptiles to spot them among the light and shade of the leaves.

The understory

Small rain forest trees, such as palms and saplings, make up the shady understory. Loops of creepers and vines cover their trunks and branches as they climb upward to reach the sunlight. Understory animals are often very mobile, using the creepers as climbing ropes to clamber into the canopy to forage for food. Some animals spend much of their time on the ground.

Sleepy sloths
The sloth spends most of its life hanging upside down from a branch, sleeping or munching on leaves. Even its shaggy fur hangs downward so that the rain drains off. Sloths live in Central and South America.

Nests and food
The blue-headed euphonia bird lives in the rain forests of South America. It flies up into the canopy to feed on mistletoe seeds, and builds its ball-shaped nest among the branches of the understory trees.

Palm civet
Small-toothed palm civets live in the rain forests of southeast Asia. Skillful climbers, they use their long claws and their tails to grip onto the trees. They feed mainly on soft fruit, such as bananas.

Emerald tree boa constrictor

The emerald tree boa constrictor from South America lies perfectly still on a branch. It looks like a vine or a bunch of leaves, until it suddenly pounces and grabs a passing bird or bat with its long front teeth. Then it squeezes its prey to death and swallows it whole.

Pretty parrots

Flocks of brilliantly colored parrots fly among the rain forest trees. The largest parrots are the macaws. Their large, curved beaks are strong enough to crack even the toughest nuts. Parrots also eat many different types of fruit.

Mushroom frogs

Many tree frogs are cleverly camouflaged to blend in with their surroundings. This makes them very difficult for hungry enemies to spot. This frog is resting on a mushroom. The honeycomb marking on the frog's skin matches the underside of the mushroom.

Orchids

Sprays of exquisite orchids dangle from the understory trees. Insects, such as bees and moths, visit the orchids to drink their sweet, syrupy nectar. As they feed, their bodies get dusted with pollen which they carry to another flower.

CROSS-SECTION OF A RAIN FOREST

Understory

Living in the shade

Very little sunlight reaches the rain forest floor, so it is always gloomy. A thick layer of decaying leaves covers the ground. Here a wide range of animals, from elephants and flightless birds, to tiny antelopes and smaller crawling creatures, hunt for food and hide. Many forest floor creatures are masters of disguise. What looks like a harmless log might turn out to be a deadly poisonous snake.

Ant gardeners

In Central and South America, tiny ants scurry across the forest floor, carrying pieces of leaves. They take the leaves to their underground nest and put them in special gardens. In the gardens, the ants grow fungus to eat.

Anteaters

This tamandua from Central and South America feeds on tiny termites. It uses its powerful claws and legs to tear open termite mounds. Then it laps up the termites with its long tongue.

Smelly flowers

The rafflesia flower smells terrible, like rotten meat. But flies think it is a tasty meal and visit it for pollination. The rafflesia grows in southeast Asia. It measures more than 3 feet across (about 1 m), making it the world's largest flower.

Forest fungi
The stinkhorn fungus from South America really lives up to its name. Its unpleasant smell attracts insects that help spread its spores. If these land in a suitable place, the spores will grow into new fungi.

Time for a bath
The tiny violet-eared hummingbird must keep its plumage in good condition to be able to fly efficiently. It preens and cleans its feathers in a stream on the forest floor.

CROSS-SECTION OF A RAIN FOREST

Forest
floor

Roots and soil
Despite the richness of growth, rain forest soil is very thin and poor. Most of the nutrition plants need to grow comes from the dead and rotting leaves covering the forest floor. Because the soil is poor, many rain forest trees grow shallow, spreading roots. These can spread over a wide area and suck up plenty of nutrition. Very tall trees grow extra roots from their trunks to stop them from falling over.

Rain frogs
Rain frogs live in the rain forests of Central and South America. Most frogs start life as eggs, turn into tadpoles, and then adults. But baby rain frogs grow inside large, clear eggs and hatch out as fully-formed frogs.

Leafy beds in the treetops

Chimpanzees live in large groups of up to 120 animals. At night, the adults build leafy nests in the trees where they will be safe from nighttime predators. Young chimps sleep with their mothers.

EUROPE

AFRICA

ATLANTIC OCEAN

INDIAN OCEAN

Rain forests grow in Central Africa along the equator. They are also found on the eastern part of Madagascar.

Reptiles in the morning

In the morning, many rain forest reptiles, like the chameleon shown below, emerge from their hiding places and climb up onto a rock or branch to bask in the sun. They need to soak in the sun's heat to make them alert and active. Then they set off to find food. As the day gets warmer, they spend less time basking in the sun and more time in the shade.

Breakfast time

Chimpanzees mainly feed on ripe forest fruits but they also eat leaves, nuts, insects, and birds. In the morning, they clamber down from their nests and begin their daylong search for food. They spend about 4 to 6 hours each day eating.

Early morning in the African rain forest

The day begins early in a tropical rain forest. As the sun's rays strike the treetops, nocturnal animals, like the deer below, settle into their dens for the day. The birds begin their dawn chorus and the daytime animals wake up and begin their search for food.

Birds and butterflies

The birds are among the first to stir, just before daybreak, and then beautiful butterflies come out to warm themselves on the leaves.

Blending in

The brightly colored rainbow lorikeet sometimes goes to sleep hanging upside down in a tree. In this position, the lorikeet looks like a bunch of leaves and can avoid its enemies. Rainbow lorikeets live in southeast Asia and Australia. They are at their most vulnerable when they are resting or when they are incubating their eggs.

An extra pair of eyes

Some rain forest creatures, like the glasswing butterfly shown here, appear to have an extra pair of eyes. The eye-like markings on their back wings help to confuse birds. A bird will probably peck at a false eye rather than a real one, and the butterfly can escape with only a slightly damaged wing.

Keeping a low profile

The rain forest is a dangerous place to live. Hungry predators lurk among the trees, on the lookout for food. Many rain forest animals have special survival skills to help them trick their enemies and stay alive. Some rely on cunning disguises. Others run for their lives, have a terrible smell, or pretend to be dead.

All shapes and sizes

In the rain forest, twigs, thorns, and leaves are not always what they seem. Many rain forest creatures hide from enemies by blending into the forest. With its blotchy brown markings and spiky horns, the horned toad from southeast Asia looks just like a wrinkled leaf on the forest floor. Not only does this hide it from enemies, it also allows the toad to ambush its prey of insects and frogs.

Hiding in the leaves

Tree frogs from South America spend the day lying perfectly still on a bromeliad plant. Their striking colors match the bromeliad's leaves and bright flowers, and help to hide the frogs from hungry lizards and birds. At night, the frogs leave their leafy roost to search for food.

Dead leaf disguise

Many rain forest insects disguise themselves as leaves, grass, or bark, to avoid predators. Their camouflage works so well that they are almost impossible to spot. The insect shown here clings to a twig, looking like a dry, dead leaf. It even sways gently in the breeze.

Playing dead

If a chameleon comes face to face with a predator, it flops over on to its side and pretends to be dead. If it is lucky, the attacker leaves it alone. Once the danger has passed, the chameleon quickly comes back to life and makes its escape.

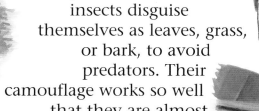

Smelly surprise

Some animals, including these rain forest butterflies, protect themselves by sending off a disgusting smell. Their odor is so bad, predators do not want to eat them.

Egg hideaway

Eggs and baby animals are particularly vulnerable to attack by predators, so some rain forest animals take extra care to protect their offspring from harm. Glass frogs from South America lay their eggs on a leaf overhanging a forest stream. They look after the eggs to keep them from drying out and being eaten by insects and birds.

Running away

The basilisk lizard lives near the river bank in the forests of Central America. If it is cornered by a predator, it has an unusual means of escape. It jumps into the river and races across the surface of the water, without falling in. Its long back legs and scaly, webbed toes stop it from sinking. When it is out of danger, it swims for the shore.

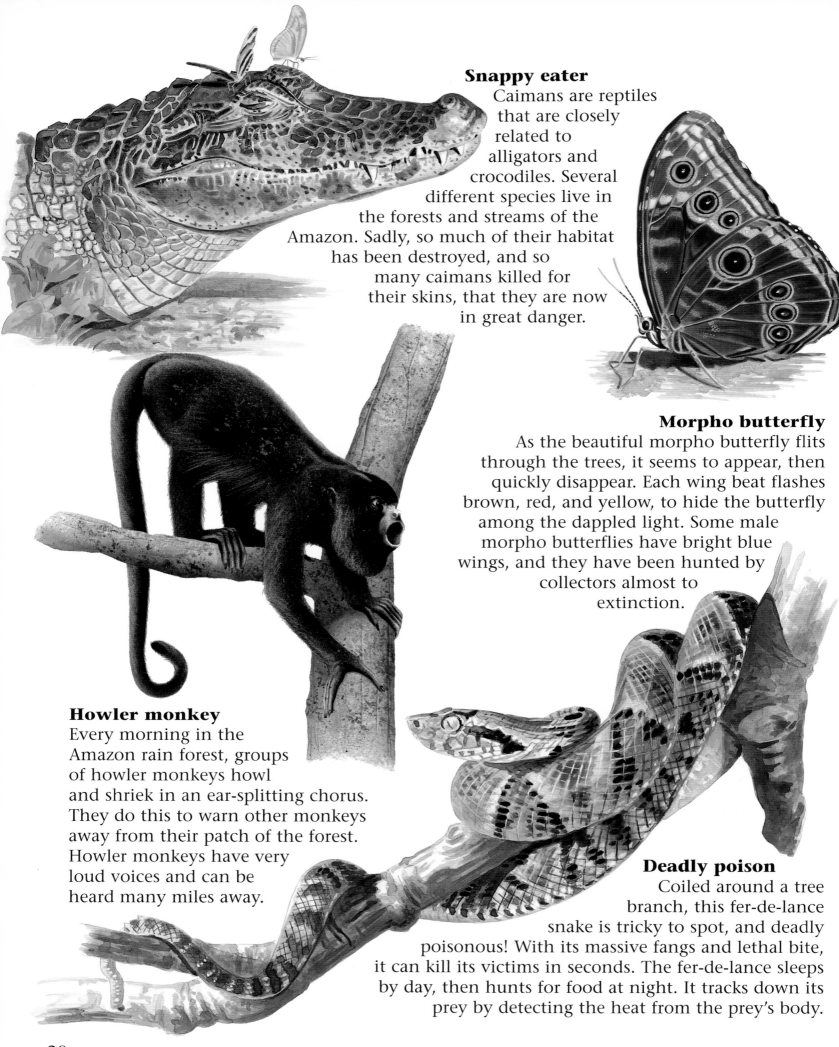

Snappy eater

Caimans are reptiles that are closely related to alligators and crocodiles. Several different species live in the forests and streams of the Amazon. Sadly, so much of their habitat has been destroyed, and so many caimans killed for their skins, that they are now in great danger.

Morpho butterfly

As the beautiful morpho butterfly flits through the trees, it seems to appear, then quickly disappear. Each wing beat flashes brown, red, and yellow, to hide the butterfly among the dappled light. Some male morpho butterflies have bright blue wings, and they have been hunted by collectors almost to extinction.

Howler monkey

Every morning in the Amazon rain forest, groups of howler monkeys howl and shriek in an ear-splitting chorus. They do this to warn other monkeys away from their patch of the forest. Howler monkeys have very loud voices and can be heard many miles away.

Deadly poison

Coiled around a tree branch, this fer-de-lance snake is tricky to spot, and deadly poisonous! With its massive fangs and lethal bite, it can kill its victims in seconds. The fer-de-lance sleeps by day, then hunts for food at night. It tracks down its prey by detecting the heat from the prey's body.

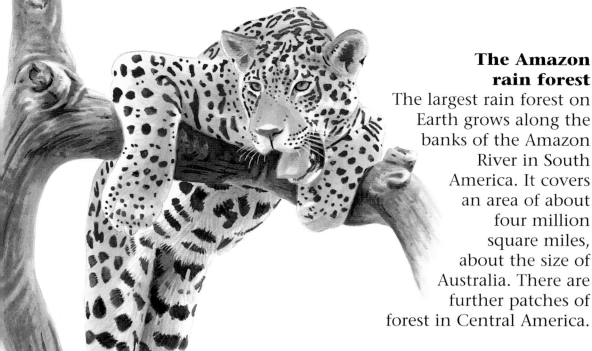

The Amazon rain forest

The largest rain forest on Earth grows along the banks of the Amazon River in South America. It covers an area of about four million square miles, about the size of Australia. There are further patches of forest in Central America.

ATLANTIC OCEAN

Amazon rain forest

PACIFIC OCEAN

SOUTH AMERICA

Hummingbirds

Tiny hummingbirds, like the sword-billed hummingbird shown below, hover in front of rain forest flowers. They poke their beaks deep inside the flowers and lap up the sugary nectar. To stay in the air, these delicate birds have to beat their wings so fast that they make a humming sound.

Dozy jaguar

During the day, a jaguar dozes in a tree, shaded from the midday sun. But at night, it is a fierce hunter, preying on birds, monkeys, and deer. It is also an excellent swimmer, and often catches fish, turtles, and caimans in the river.

Fruit feeders

The loud squawking of parrots disturbs the quiet of the rain forest. Colorful flocks of parrots fly through the trees, feeding on rain forest fruit.

High noon in the Amazon rain forest

At noon in the rain forest, it is hot, steamy, and eerily quiet. Many rain forest animals spend the day asleep, lazing by the riverbank or dozing in the shade. As the afternoon draws on, towering black storm clouds gather overhead. There is a crash of thunder, and a flash of lightning; the forest is in for its daily soaking.

Killers

Danger lurks everywhere in the rain forest as deadly killers hunt and catch their prey. Some track their victims by daylight, using their superb eyesight. Others are nocturnal predators, relying on their senses of hearing or smell to find their prey in the dark. Prey animals can turn into killers, too, as they try to protect themselves.

Deadly snakes

Some rain forest snakes are deadly poisonous. They strike at their prey with their long, front fangs and inject them with lethal poison. Other snakes, like the ringed tree boa shown here, have another sinister way of hunting. This boa stuns its prey with a blow to the head, then it coils itself around the prey and squeezes it to death. The prey is swallowed whole, head first.

Sting in the tail

Some rain forest scorpions have stingers in their tails, loaded with deadly poison. They mainly use these lethal weapons in self-defense, curling their tails over their head, ready to strike. Some scorpions can kill humans. Their stings cause breathing problems, agonizing pain, and finally, death.

Black caiman

The black caiman from South America is the largest caiman, growing up to 15 feet (4.5 m) long. It lurks unseen in the water, with just its eyes and nostrils poking up. Any passing fish, birds, or small mammals are quickly snapped up in the caiman's sharp, pointed teeth.

Fierce fish

Armed with rows of razor-sharp teeth, piranhas are the deadliest fish in the South American rain forest. They usually prey on other fish but may attack larger animals, such as tapirs and cows, that come to the water to drink. A school of piranha can strip an animal to the bone in minutes.

Harpy eagle

The harpy eagle is one of the most powerful birds of prey in the world. Swooping low over the forest, it uses its strong talons to wrench monkeys and other animals from the treetops. It lives in the wildest, most isolated parts of the forests.

Bird-eating spiders

The South American goliath bird-eating spider shown here is the world's largest spider. Including its long hairy legs, it can grow as large as a dinner plate. It comes out a night to hunt for prey, lies in wait, and then pounces. It injects its prey with poison that causes paralysis.

Tiger hunter

A tiger's stripes help to hide it among the undergrowth as it stalks its prey of cattle or deer. When the tiger is within range, it pounces and brings down its prey with its huge front claws. Then it kills its victim with a lethal bite. Tigers live in the rain forests of Asia.

Poison-arrow frogs

The poison-arrow frog's brightly colored skin is a signal to its enemies. It warns them that this frog is very bad to eat. Its skin contains a poison so deadly that one tiny drop could kill a monkey instantly. Local hunters in South America extract the frogs' poison and use it to tip their hunting arrows.

23

Cats' eyes
The green cat snake shown here mainly lives among the trees overhanging the water. Its eyes are adapted for seeing at night when it comes out to hunt for tree-dwelling lizards and frogs. It injects its prey with powerful poison before swallowing it whole.

Tapir markings
The Malaysian tapir's striking black and white coat helps to hide it among the light and shadows on the forest floor. Tapirs are shy and secretive. They come out at night to browse on shoots, buds, and leaves.

INDIA

Indochinese peninsula

INDIAN OCEAN

INDONESIA

PACIFIC OCEAN

Asian rain forests
This map shows where the Asian rain forests are located. Patches of rain forest are found from India into the countries of southeast Asia.

A place to sleep
Orangutans live in the rain forests of Borneo and Sumatra. These intelligent apes spend the day in the lower branches of the trees, searching for food. At night, they build a sleeping nest in the trees, choosing a new site each night. The nest is woven from branches and leaves, and has a sturdy base and roof.

Dusk in an Asian rain forest

Night falls quickly in the rain forest. At about six o'clock, the forest grows dark. There are no twilight hours of dusk. As the sun sets, daytime animals go back to their dens or nests, and a new group of animals wakes up and begins to search for food. This split into day and night means that there is plenty of food and territory to go around.

Bats in action

As night falls in the forest, thousands of shadows flit among the trees. Bats spend the day roosting in trees and caves. At night, they fly out to look for food. Some bats feed on moths and other insects, swooping down to catch them in midair. Others are fruit-eaters, using their keen sense of smell to locate ripe fruit.

Sun bear

By day, the sun bear from southeast Asia rests or sunbathes in the trees on a bed of bent-over branches. At night, it climbs down to the ground to feed on small mammals and termites.

Flying frogs

In the rain forests of Asia, there are lizards, snakes, and even frogs that are able to glide from tree to tree. To escape from a predator, the flying frog stretches out the webs of skin between its fingers and toes. Then it glides through the air like a tiny parachute.

Proboscis monkey

The proboscis monkey gets its name from the male's huge, bulging nose (or proboscis). The male uses its nose as a loudspeaker to boost the sound of its warning honk. If the male gets excited or angry, its nose inflates and turns red, like a balloon being blown up.

25

Rain forest babies

Rain forests are the richest habitats on Earth, overflowing with all kinds of animals. Because there are no seasons, rain forest babies are hatched or born throughout the year. Some youngsters spend the first part of their lives with their parents, who feed them, protect them from predators, and teach them how to fend for themselves.

Hanging on

Animal parents cannot always be with their offspring. In Africa, this tiny bush baby's mother has gone hunting. Before leaving, the female placed the baby on a twig where it will wait until she comes back with food.

Hatching out

Most reptiles, such as the lizard shown here, hatch from eggs. The mother lays her eggs in a place safe from predators. When the baby reptiles hatch, they must care for themselves.

Taking off

The big moment for baby birds comes when they leave their nest and fly off on their own. This hummingbird fledgling from South America is ready for its first flight.

Loving parents

African bullfrogs keep their babies safe by carrying them on their bodies. Some rain forest parents take care of their offspring for months or even years after they are born. Other parents simply lay their eggs, or give birth to their young, and then leave them to cope on their own.

Elephant families
Elephants have a very strong sense of family. A group of elephants is led by a matriarch (the female in charge) and is made up of other females and their young. The female elephants help each other to give birth and to look after their young.

Growing up
Many rain forest babies look like miniature versions of their parents when they are born. Others gradually acquire the shape and colors of a fully-grown adult. This young mandrill from Africa is beginning to show the bright colors of the adult male on his muzzle.

Asian elephants, like this newborn baby and its mother, feed on trees and plants in the rain forest.

Learning to survive
Collared peccaries live in Central and South America. They are distantly related to wild hogs. Baby peccaries, like the one shown above, stay with their mothers for about two months after they are born. During that time, they learn how to locate the best foods and how to defend themselves from predators.

Baby jumbos
Elephants have the longest gestation period (pregnancy) of any animal. It takes 22 months for the baby to grow large enough inside its mother to be born. Although smaller than their African cousins, a newborn baby Asian elephant still weighs in at between 200 and 250 pounds (between 90 and 113 kg).

Night in the Australian rain forest

The pitch black of the rain forest night is the time for the nocturnal animals to be out and about. Moths take over for butterflies, bats replace birds, and nighttime hunters take advantage of the cover of darkness to prowl the forest floor. Nocturnal animals are perfectly adapted to life in the dark. Extra-sharp hearing and keen eyesight help them to navigate and to find their food.

Tree-climbing kangaroos

Some tree kangaroos can still hop on the ground, but most are adapted for life in the trees. They have sharp, curved claws for climbing, and they forage for leaves and fruit. The Lumholtz's tree kangaroo shown here spends the day sleeping, curled up in the fork of a high branch.

INDIAN OCEAN

AUSTRALIA

Tasmania

The three main patches of tropical rain forest in Australia grow along the northeast coast. Much of the island of New Guinea to the north is covered in thick forest.

Ghostly bats

The deathly pale Australian ghost bat flies silently through the forest, looking for insects to eat. It uses echolocation to navigate and find its prey. The bat makes a series of high-pitched noises. If the sounds hit a solid object, they send back an echo that the bat's large, sensitive ears pick up. From the echo, the bat can tell what the object is.

Night-flying insects

By day, huge butterflies fly through the forest, feeding on flower nectar. At night, their place is taken by moths which hover in front of flowers and drink nectar through their long, straw-like tongues. The flowers on which the moths feed only open at night because they rely on the moths for pollination. The moths themselves may be preyed upon by birds and mammals.

Dangerous birds

The cassowary is a large, flightless bird that lives in New Guinea and Australia. Its toes are armed with dagger-sharp claws for striking at enemies. A well-aimed kick from a cassowary can be fatal to a human being. The bony helmet on the cassowary's head is used for pushing through undergrowth and turning over the leaf litter to find food.

Rain forest plants

Tropical rain forests cover less than ten percent of the earth's surface, but they contain almost half of its known species of plants. There is no winter near the equator where tropical rain forests occur, so plants can grow and reproduce all year round. These conditions have created a huge variety of trees, vines, ferns, and epiphytes.

Flying seeds

The alsomitra is a vine that grows in the tropical forests of Asia. Its seeds (above) have a light, transparent wing about 6 inches (15 cm) long that allows them to glide long distances before they reach the ground. In this way, the new plant can grow a long way from its mother-plant.

Floating seeds

Coconuts are the fruit and seeds of coconut palms that grow near the sea in tropical regions. Due to the special fiber that covers them, these large seeds (weighing up to 40 pounds or 18 kg) can float for a long time, far away from their place of origin. Once they reach a new beach, they begin to germinate and bear fruit after seven or eight years.

Giant water lily

Giant water lilies have massive leaves, strong enough for a child to sit on. The leaves are full of air-filled spaces that keep them afloat. The water lilies grow in the Amazon River.

Tiny ecosystems

Bromeliaceae (left) are a type of air-plant that grows on trees in tropical forests in Central and South America. Where the rainwater collects inside their leaves, tiny lakes form. Insects, frogs, and other animals come to live there. Reptiles, birds, and mammals visit the plants to drink the water and feed on the animals. This great wealth of life makes the Bromeliaceae true miniature ecosystems.

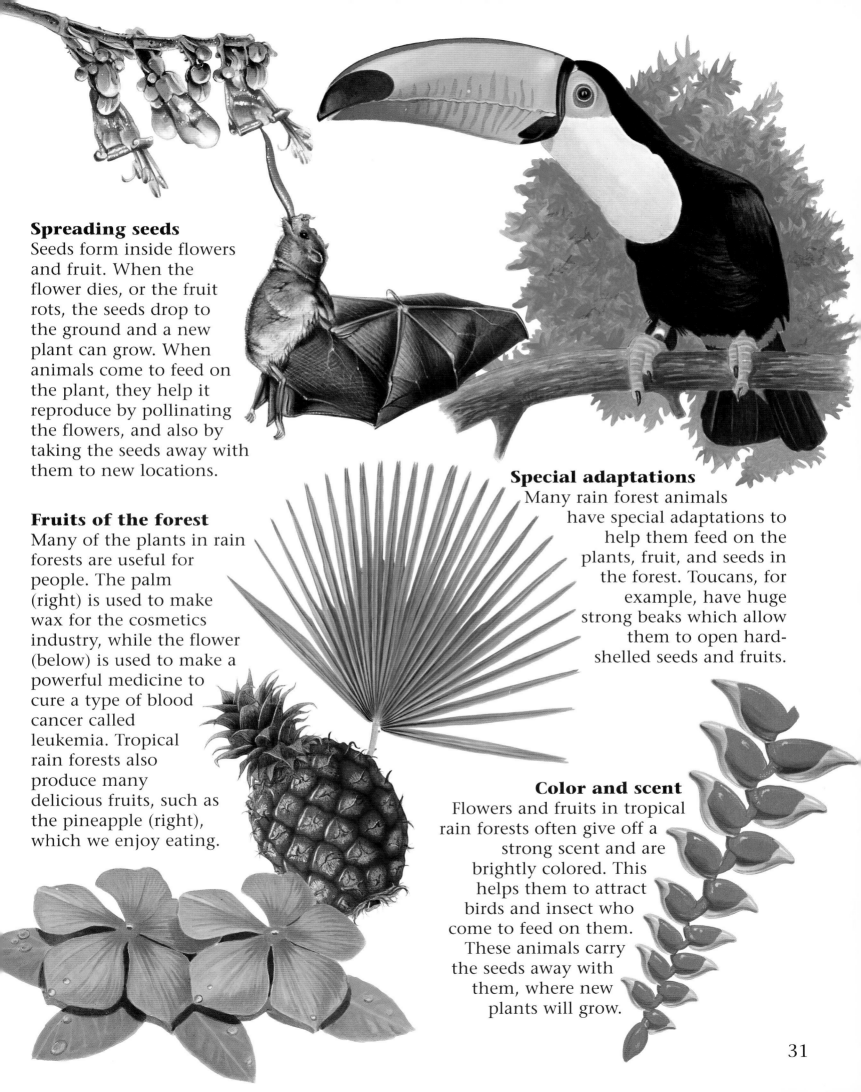

Spreading seeds

Seeds form inside flowers and fruit. When the flower dies, or the fruit rots, the seeds drop to the ground and a new plant can grow. When animals come to feed on the plant, they help it reproduce by pollinating the flowers, and also by taking the seeds away with them to new locations.

Fruits of the forest

Many of the plants in rain forests are useful for people. The palm (right) is used to make wax for the cosmetics industry, while the flower (below) is used to make a powerful medicine to cure a type of blood cancer called leukemia. Tropical rain forests also produce many delicious fruits, such as the pineapple (right), which we enjoy eating.

Special adaptations

Many rain forest animals have special adaptations to help them feed on the plants, fruit, and seeds in the forest. Toucans, for example, have huge strong beaks which allow them to open hard-shelled seeds and fruits.

Color and scent

Flowers and fruits in tropical rain forests often give off a strong scent and are brightly colored. This helps them to attract birds and insect who come to feed on them. These animals carry the seeds away with them, where new plants will grow.

31

Destroying the planet's "lungs"

Rain forests are the "lungs" of our planet. They absorb large quantities of carbon dioxide and release oxygen. The widespread practice of burning off or cutting down the forests releases even more carbon dioxide into the atmosphere. Increasing amounts of carbon dioxide are responsible for higher temperatures and global warming.

Animals in danger

One of the most seriously endangered forest animals is the golden lion tamarin shown here. This beautiful creature lives in a few patches of forest in coastal Brazil. So much of its habitat has been destroyed, and so many tamarins illegally collected for the pet trade, that only a few hundred are left. Captive breeding programs set up in Europe and in the United States are helping to release tamarins back into the wild.

Rain forests in danger

At the beginning of the 20th century, tropical rain forests covered twice as much of the earth as they do today. Every year, an area of rain forest the size of Switzerland is destroyed. Rain forest animals have less and less space to live in and many have already become extinct. Many indigenous people also make their homes in the forests. Their traditional ways of life are threatened as they are forced to leave their homes.

Saving the forests

All over the world, conservation groups, such as the WWF (World Wildlife Fund), The Rain Forest Foundation, and RAN (The Rain Forest Action Network) are working hard to save the forests before it is too late. They campaign to establish protected nature reserves and parks, and to safeguard the future of wildlife and people.

Destroying the forests

There are many reasons why the rain forests are being destroyed. Timber from rain forest trees, such as teak or mahogany, is sold to wealthy countries for millions of dollars. Gold and other precious minerals have been found deep in the forest. Farmers and ranchers cut down and burn trees to clear plots of land. The problem is that any nutrients in the rain forest soil are quickly used up and the farmers soon have to move on and start again.

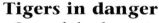

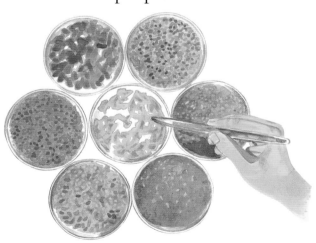

Replanting the forests

Scientists all over the world are working to understand the botany of rain forests so that they can develop new seeds and plants to refurbish the forests more effectively. This illustration shows an experiment in a laboratory in Milan, Italy.

Tigers in danger

One of the largest surviving groups of wild tigers lives in the Sundarbans, a huge mangrove forest in southwest Bangladesh. Elsewhere, tigers are extremely rare, having been hunted almost to extinction for their bones and skins. Some now live in special forest reserves with guards to protect them from poachers.

1. How high do rain forest trees grow?
2. What is another name for an epiphyte?
3. How many rain forest animals live in the canopy?
4. What does a chameleon do when it sees a predator?
5. Where do rain frogs live?
6. Name three animals that live in the understory.
7. How much time do chimpanzees spend eating?
8. When are rain forest babies born?
9. How did the proboscis monkey get its name?

10. Where do orangutans live?
11. What is the understory?
12. Where are tropical rain forests found?
13. Which bird eats mistletoe seeds?
14. Does a jaguar hunt by day or by night?
15. What is the largest parrot in the rain forest?
16. What do chimpanzees eat?
17. Why do many flowers and fruits give off strong scents and have such bright colors?
18. How much rain forest is destroyed each year?

START

THE TROPICAL RAIN FOREST GAME

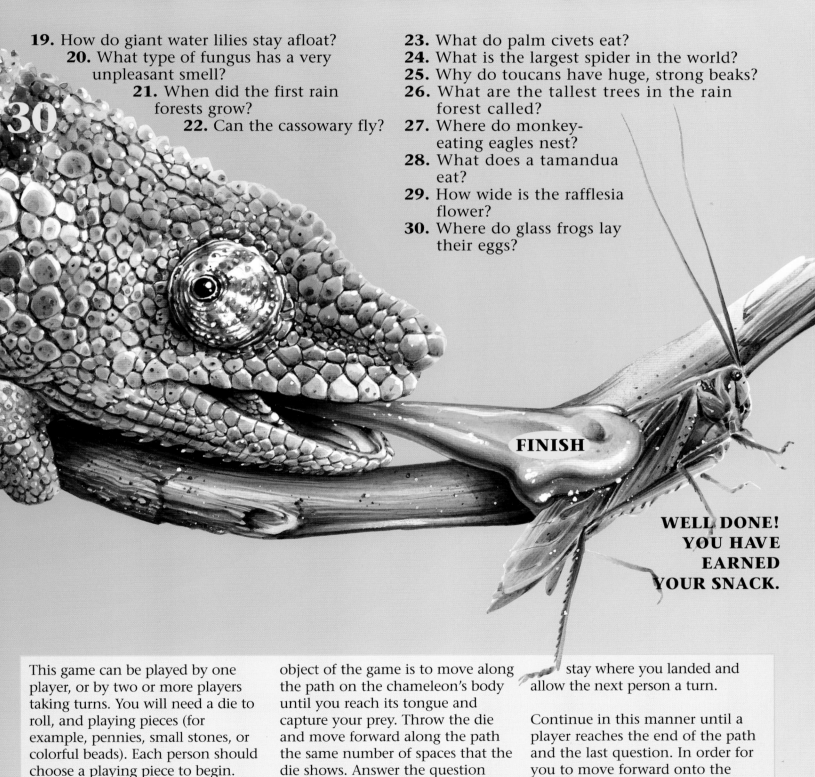

19. How do giant water lilies stay afloat?
20. What type of fungus has a very unpleasant smell?
21. When did the first rain forests grow?
22. Can the cassowary fly?

30

23. What do palm civets eat?
24. What is the largest spider in the world?
25. Why do toucans have huge, strong beaks?
26. What are the tallest trees in the rain forest called?
27. Where do monkey-eating eagles nest?
28. What does a tamandua eat?
29. How wide is the rafflesia flower?
30. Where do glass frogs lay their eggs?

FINISH

**WELL DONE!
YOU HAVE
EARNED
YOUR SNACK.**

This game can be played by one player, or by two or more players taking turns. You will need a die to roll, and playing pieces (for example, pennies, small stones, or colorful beads). Each person should choose a playing piece to begin.

You are a hungry chameleon! The object of the game is to move along the path on the chameleon's body until you reach its tongue and capture your prey. Throw the die and move forward along the path the same number of spaces that the die shows. Answer the question correctly and you may take another turn. If you answer incorrectly, stay where you landed and allow the next person a turn.

Continue in this manner until a player reaches the end of the path and the last question. In order for you to move forward onto the chameleon's tongue, you must answer the last question correctly.

Answers to the game

1. Some trees can grow as tall as a twenty-story building.

2. Epiphytes are also called air-plants.

3. About two-thirds of rain forest animals live in the canopy.

4. A chameleon flops over on to its side and pretends to be dead when it sees a predator.

5. Rain frogs live in the rain forests of Central and South America.

6. Animals that live in the understory may include the sloth, the iguana, the euphonia, the sun bear, the emerald boa constrictor, the mushroom frog, the palm civet, and the parrot.

7. Chimpanzees spend about 4 to 6 hours each day eating.

8. Rain forest babies are hatched or born throughout the year.

9. The proboscis monkey gets its name from the male's huge, bulging nose (or proboscis).

10. Orangutans live in the rain forests of Borneo and Sumatra.

11. The understory is the area below the canopy where trees and saplings grow.

12. Tropical rain forests are found near the equator in regions with high rainfall and hot, steamy climates.

13. The blue-headed euphonia bird eats mistletoe seeds.

14. A jaguar hunts by night.

15. The largest parrot in the rain forest is the macaw.

16. Chimpanzees mainly feed on ripe fruits but they also eat leaves, nuts, insects, and birds.

17. The strong scents and bright colors of the fruit and flowers are designed to attract birds and insects who carry the seeds away with them, where new plants will grow.

18. Every year an area of rain forest about the size of Switzerland is destroyed.

19. The leaves of the giant water lily are full of air-filled spaces which keep them afloat.

20. The stinkhorn fungus has a very unpleasant smell.

21. The first rain forests grew about 150 million years ago.

22. No. The cassowary is a large flightless bird.

23. Palm civets feed mainly on soft fruit, such as bananas.

24. The South American goliath bird-eating spider is the largest spider in the world.

25. Toucans have huge strong beaks so they can open hard-shelled seeds and fruit.

26. The tallest trees in the rain forests are called emergents.

27. Monkey-eating eagles nest in the treetops.

28. A tamandua eats termites.

29. The rafflesia flower measures more than 3 feet across (about 1 m).

30. Glass frogs lay their eggs on leaves overhanging forest streams.

Glossary

browse: to feed on leaves, twigs, and sparse vegetation.

canopy: the thick, green roof over the rain forest. It contains a dense mass of branches, leaves, flowers, and fruit, and is warm and wet because it gets most of the sun and rain.

camouflage: the colors and patterns on something that match or blend in with its surroundings.

carnivore: meat-eating animals, like the tiger.

diurnal animals: animals that are active by day and sleep at night, such as the lion.

echolocation: a type of radar used by bats to navigate and find their prey. They make a series of high-pitched noises. If the sounds hit a solid object, they send back an echo that the bats' large, sensitive ears pick up.

ecosystem: a place where animals and plants live and interact with their environment and with each other.

equator: an imaginary line that runs around the center of the earth.

forage: to search for food.

habitat: the natural home of plants or animals.

herbivores: animals, like the palm civet, that only eat plants.

matriarch: the female in charge of finding food and water for the herd.

mammals: animals, like chimpanzees, that give birth to their young and raise them on the mother's milk. Mammals are usually covered in fur or hair.

nectar: a sweet liquid found in plants that many insects and birds feed on.

nocturnal animals: animals that are active by night and sleep in the day, like the jaguar.

plumage: a bird's feathers.

pollen: the fine powder in a flower that helps it to reproduce. The pollen is carried away by birds, insects, and the wind to other flowers where it fertilizes their seeds.

predator: animals, like the caiman, that kill other animals for food.

proboscis: the elongated part of the mouth of animals or insects, like an elephant's trunk.

roost: to settle down to sleep, or perch for the night.

reptile: cold-blooded animals, like a chameleon, that usually lay eggs.

saplings: young trees.

species: groups of plants or animals that have the same features and that can reproduce within their groups.

spores: tiny male reproductive cells in plants like ferns, mosses, or fungi.

tropics: the region between the Tropic of Cancer (north of the equator) and the Tropic of Capricorn (south of the equator).

undergrowth: shrubs and small trees growing under larger ones.

understory: the place in the rain forest where the trees and saplings grow. It is below the canopy.

Index